GW01336653

Origins

The Gas in your Home
The Paper in your Home
A Spoonful of Sugar
Wool for Warmth
A Cup of Tea
Rubber Tyres on your Bike
The Water in your Tap
A Loaf of Bread
A Cup of Coffee
The Meat in your Hamburger

First published in 1982 by Wayland Publishers Limited
49 Lansdowne Place, Hove,
East Sussex BN3 1HF, England
© Copyright 1982 Wayland Publishers Limited
ISBN 0 85340 942 0

Illustrated by Malcolm Walker
Typeset by Computacomp (UK) Ltd
Fort William, Scotland
Printed in Italy by G. Canale & C.S.p.A., Turin
Bound in the U.K. by The Pitman Press, Bath

A Cup of TEA

ANDREW LANGLEY

Wayland

A cup of tea

In Laura's house they drink a lot of tea. As soon as her father gets up, he brews a pot and brings a cup to Laura and one to her mother. In the middle of the morning, and again in the afternoon, Laura's mother puts the kettle on to make more tea. When her father comes home from work, the first thing he asks for is a cup of tea!

Tea is one of the best-loved drinks in the world. People living in places as far apart as Britain and Australia, or South America and Japan, all like to drink several cups a day. They like it because it is refreshing, especially when they are tired or upset. It is also cheap to buy.

Laura asked her mother why a cup of tea always makes her feel wide awake in the morning. Her mother said it was because of a substance in the tea called caffeine, which makes people feel more lively. A small amount can be good for you, but too much will give you a headache.

Laura's father told her that where he worked there were special breaks for tea in the morning and the afternoon. The cups of tea were bought from a machine. If money is put in the slot and a button pressed, the machine pours the tea into a plastic cup. He didn't think it tasted as nice as the tea at home!

How to brew tea

When Laura's friend Bill came round to play, Laura asked her mother if she could make some tea. She filled the kettle and put it on the stove to heat up. Before it had boiled, her mother told her to pour some of the hot water into the teapot to warm it, because, she said, "a warm pot makes better tea".

Then the hot water in the teapot was emptied out, and Laura put the tea leaves in—one spoonful for each person, and one for the pot. This makes strong tea. If you are using good quality tea leaves, you should put in less.

As soon as the kettle began to boil, Laura took the pot over to the stove and poured in the boiling water. Before she poured it into the cups, she left the mixture to 'brew' for about five minutes. During this time, the leaves are softened by the hot water, and give out their flavour and colouring.

Buying tea from the shops

One day, Laura's mother asked Laura and Bill to go out and buy her some more tea. In the shop, they found it hard to choose which packet to buy. They had always thought that all tea was the same, but the shopkeeper told them that there were many different kinds. The most popular tea comes from India and Sri Lanka, and is generally known as 'Indian'. China tea usually has a more delicate flavour and must not be brewed too strong.

Some people find it easier and less messy to use tea bags. The tea leaves are sealed in a tiny paper bag, which has holes to let the water in and the flavour out. Although tea bags are usually filled with low-quality leaves and are more expensive than loose tea, they certainly make washing up much easier.

The shopkeeper said that there was even a kind of instant tea which could be made like instant coffee, just by pouring on hot water and adding milk. These are what are used in tea and coffee machines, like the one where Laura's father works.

The job of the blender

When we buy a packet of tea, we expect it to taste exactly the same as the last one we bought. Each tea firm tries to make sure that its brand has the same flavour and aroma all the time. But this is not as easy as it sounds. There will be a difference in taste between those leaves which are grown early in the year, and those which are grown late. Tea grown on the top of a hill is different from that grown in a valley.

So almost all the tea we buy is a mixture of many kinds of leaf. This mixing—called blending—is a very skilled job, and the blender is an important person in the tea firm. He must be able to tell the difference between teas from their taste, smell and appearance, and then decide on the right amounts to mix together.

The blender will sip teas brewed from each of the available kinds of leaf—there may be as many as thirty of these. Then he will write down a recipe which will produce the right taste. Although the taste must be exactly right, most of the blend will be made up with a 'filler'. This is a cheap tea which has hardly any taste of its own. By using a filler, the blender does not need to use so much of the more expensive and tasty tea. This is one reason why tea is still so cheap to buy.

How tea is packed

As long as tea is kept in an airtight packet, it will stay fresh. But as soon as the packet is opened, the dry leaves will begin to soak up dampness from the air. If the tea is left open to the air, it will soon lose its taste and be spoilt. So it is important that the tea is packed as soon as possible.

If the tea has to be blended, the different kinds of leaf are fed into a large drum according to the blender's recipe. The drum spins so that the tea is properly mixed.

Next, the tea is poured onto a moving belt and passed through a sieve, which removes any large pieces of leaf or dirt. Leaves which are too small—the dust—are blown off by a fan. The tea also passes over a magnet, just in case any pieces of metal from the tea chest, in which it was packed, have got into the mixture. Finally, it is poured into cardboard packets, where it is pressed down and sealed in. These packets usually hold only a small amount of tea—about 100g—so that the customer does not have to buy too much at once.

Usually the tea 'dust' is used for making tea bags. A small amount—about the same as one teaspoonful—is sealed inside a paper bag. The paper is specially made so that it does not go soggy when it is wet.

Buying and selling tea

Because tea soon loses its freshness it must be transported from the place where it is grown and sold to the tea firms as quickly as possible. The firms need to have a regular supply of tea throughout the year because they do not store it for very long.

The tea is bought and sold at special sales, called auctions, which are held every week. When the tea arrives by boat from the country where it was grown, it is stored in a warehouse. Samples of each kind of tea are taken and sent away to the firms who may wish to buy.

who makes notes. The taster is often a busy man—he may have to sample as many as 700 different brews in one day! He never swallows any of the liquid, but spits it out into a bowl.

Each tea firm will send a buyer to the auction, who will bid for the teas that the taster has chosen. Anyone is allowed to bid at the auctions—even a member of the public can bid, as long as he has enough money.

Tasting the samples and choosing which ones to buy is the job of the taster, who is just as important as the blender. He works in a big tasting room, where he moves along a line of small bowls, each containing freshly-brewed tea. He takes a sip of the tea with a spoon, then looks at the tea leaves carefully, passing on his report about each tea to his assistant,

Taking tea around the world

Tea can only be grown successfully in hot countries. But it is drunk by people all over the world, and often has to be carried huge distances before it can be blended and put into packets. Tea is easy to transport because the dried leaves are very light. The tea is packed in special square boxes called tea chests, made of wood. Tea chests have been used for many years, because they are cheap to make and easy to stack.

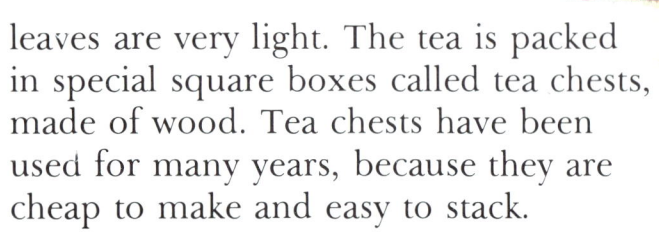

As we have seen, the tea must be kept dry or it will be unfit to sell. So the chests are lined on the inside with aluminium foil, which keeps the air out. When they are full, the lid is nailed down tightly.

Most tea is transported by sea. The chests are taken to the nearest port and loaded into the hold of a cargo ship, which will carry them to the tea-drinking countries.

Sorting out the sizes

Of course, the leaves that we buy in a packet are not the same size as the leaves that grow on the tea bush. They have been broken up into small pieces. But the pieces are of many different sizes and, before the tea can be packed in the chest, it must be sifted and graded.

The tea passes over a series of mesh sieves, which shake so that the leaves fall through. The first sieve has the widest holes, and gets rid of any pieces of stalk or dirt. The finer sieves sort the leaves into different sizes. After the tea has been sorted it is poured into separate bins. The largest size is called broken leaf, and usually makes the best tea. Next are the fannings, and smallest of all is the tea dust.

Why is tea black?

Almost all of the tea that we drink is black. But when the tea leaves are picked from the bush they are green, like any other leaves. They only turn black because of a special process called fermenting. This takes place in rooms which are kept cool and slightly damp. The leaves are spread out on large aluminium trays.

Fermenting takes about three hours to complete. During this time, the oxygen in the air is absorbed into the leaf, which turns dark brown. The juices which give tea its flavour, form a sticky liquid on the surface of the leaf.

The next step is to dry the tea quickly, so that the juice dries on the outside of the leaf. The trays are carried on a moving belt into a drying chamber, where hot air is blown in. The heat makes the leaves crisp and dry, and stops them from fermenting any further.

When we pour boiling water on the tea, we are simply wetting it again and allowing the juices to soak off.

Although the tea is now dry, the taste and aroma will go on developing for two or three weeks.

Mincing and rolling the leaf

Before it can ferment, the tea leaf has to be broken up and slightly crushed. This squeezes the juices out, and allows the oxygen in the air to be absorbed quickly and evenly.

There are several ways of breaking up the leaves. The most common is by rolling them. The leaves are pressed into a drum over a revolving table, which twists and breaks the leaves and squeezes out the juice. Great care is taken to make sure that the juice does not run away—it is collected in a tray below the machine and returned to the tea leaves. During the rolling, the tea will become slightly hotter and this speeds up the fermentation.

Many tea factories now use a Crushing, Tearing and Curling Machine—called CTC for short. This is rather like a big mangle, made of two rollers with rough surfaces. One turns very fast, and the other turns quite slowly. The leaves are fed between the two rollers, and are twisted and torn, releasing the juices.

Sometimes the tea leaves are first minced up in a machine called a Rotorvane. This is a large drum, with sharp 'vanes' or rotating knives inside. The tea leaves are pressed into it, and chopped into small pieces.

Drying and withering

When the leaves are freshly-picked, they must first of all be partly dried out. This is called withering and is an important part of teamaking. If the leaves have too much moisture in them, they may go rotten instead of fermenting.

At the end of the day, the plucked leaves are brought in from the fields. They are spread out in thin layers on long racks made of nylon mesh. Warm air is blown through the troughs underneath the racks, removing most of the moisture from the leaves.

Some other ways of making tea

Not all tea is black. In the East, many people prefer drinking green tea, which is made from leaves which have not been fermented. After they are plucked, the green leaves are heated in an iron pan over a charcoal fire. They quickly turn yellow, and the chemicals which cause fermentation are killed. The leaves can then be rolled in the same way as black tea. Tea made from these leaves is green and tastes bitter, but the Japanese and Chinese like it that way!

In Tibet, the tea leaves are pressed together into a hard brick. When Tibetans want to make tea, they cut off pieces and boil it up into a kind of stew. In Burma the leaves are eaten as a vegetable. They are steamed and then buried in a bamboo-lined pit for six months. When the tea is dug up, it is pickled, and eaten to give energy for a hard day's work.

Plucking the leaves

Tea is harvested throughout the warmer months of the year. Because only a few leaves are taken each time and because tea bushes grow very fast, each bush can be plucked as often as once a week. In a whole season, one bush will produce enough young leaves to make about 2kgs of tea.

Only the youngest and juiciest leaves on the bush are plucked. Usually the bud and the top two leaves are taken, but sometimes three or four leaves may be taken for lower quality teas.

The plucking is done by an army of workers. They must be careful not to bruise the leaves when they pick them, as tea leaves quickly spoil if they are crushed. The leaves are thrown into baskets held by a strap round the plucker's head or shoulders. When the basket is full it is carefully weighed. The more baskets that are filled, the more the plucker will be paid.

Many people have tried to build machines to pluck the tea bushes faster than human fingers, but none of these have been successful. Machines bruise the leaves and they cannot choose the right buds and leaves to pick.

Pruning the bushes

If left to themselves, the tea bushes would grow into large trees with tough leaves, and they would be difficult to pluck. The bushes are kept small by careful and regular cutting, so that they stay the right height for the pluckers—about one metre from the ground.

This cutting is called pruning, and has to be done very skilfully. The top of the bush is pruned flat, so that the best leaves can easily be seen and picked. This is called the 'plucking table'. Pruning also encourages plenty of tender new shoots to grow.

Helping the tea to grow

Tea can only be grown in hot countries where there is no frost to harm the bushes. But there must also be enough rain to help them grow, and the air should be damp and hot, but not scorching. The best tea comes from the hill country of tropical lands, safe from strong winds and storms.

Pests and diseases can cause a lot of damage to tea plantations. Fungus can attack the leaves and roots, and beetles and mites can burrow inside the stems of the plants. Most growers do not like to spray the bushes with chemicals, as it will spoil the taste and harm the soil. They will only use chemical sprays if the damage is serious.

The soil itself also has to be kept healthy, by feeding it with compost, such as the prunings from the bushes. Many tea growers also spread a factory-made fertilizer on their soil every year.

New plants from old

There are two ways of growing a new tea bush. The first, of course, is by sowing the seed and growing a seedling. But where do the seeds come from? We have seen how a tea bush, if it is not pruned, will grow into a tree. It will also produce flowers, and these in turn will produce seeds.

There are never any flowers on a bush which has been pruned for plucking. The seeds are taken from bushes specially grown and allowed to flower, in what is called the 'seed garden'. The seeds are sown indoors, sheltered from cold and wind. When the little plants are three years old, they are strong enough to be planted outside in rows.

The other way of growing a new bush is by taking a cutting from a 'mother' bush. A strong shoot is cut from a healthy bush and planted in a sheltered spot. Soon it will grow roots of its own and become a baby tea plant.

Bushes grown in this way are usually stronger and more productive than those grown from seed. By taking cuttings from a strong, high-yielding plant, the grower can be sure that the little plants will be just as strong as their 'mother'.

Who drinks tea...?

Everyone knows that the British love tea. So it is not surprising to find that they drink far more than anyone else—an average of six cups each every day! Nearly a third of all the tea that is exported around the world goes to Great Britain and Ireland.

Black tea is by far the most popular tea. But people drink it in all sorts of different ways. Many people like to drink it with lemon. The British pour milk into it; Russians like jam in it; Eskimos boil the leaves for about ten minutes, instead of letting their tea brew; Tibetans like their tea churned up with butter, and Koreans serve theirs with raw eggs and rice cakes. In North America it is often served cold, as a summer drink.

Tea has a very important place in Japanese life. Before their famous tea-drinking ceremony, Japanese guests are invited to walk in the garden so that they will be quiet and relaxed. The tea, which is always green, is brewed and served in a special room, where the guests kneel on the floor and slowly sip the drink.

... and who grows it?

India produces more tea than any other country, mostly grown in the hills of the north. It is almost all black tea, and the most famous comes from Darjeeling, high up in the Himalayas. There are also large plantations for black tea in Bangladesh, Sri Lanka, Java and Sumatra.

China is also a very large producer of tea. The flavour of China tea is quite different to that of Indian tea. The well known *Souchong* teas have a delicate smoky taste. A lot of green tea is also grown in China, and in Japan green tea is the only kind to be grown.

Tea is grown on plantations in many countries all over the world.

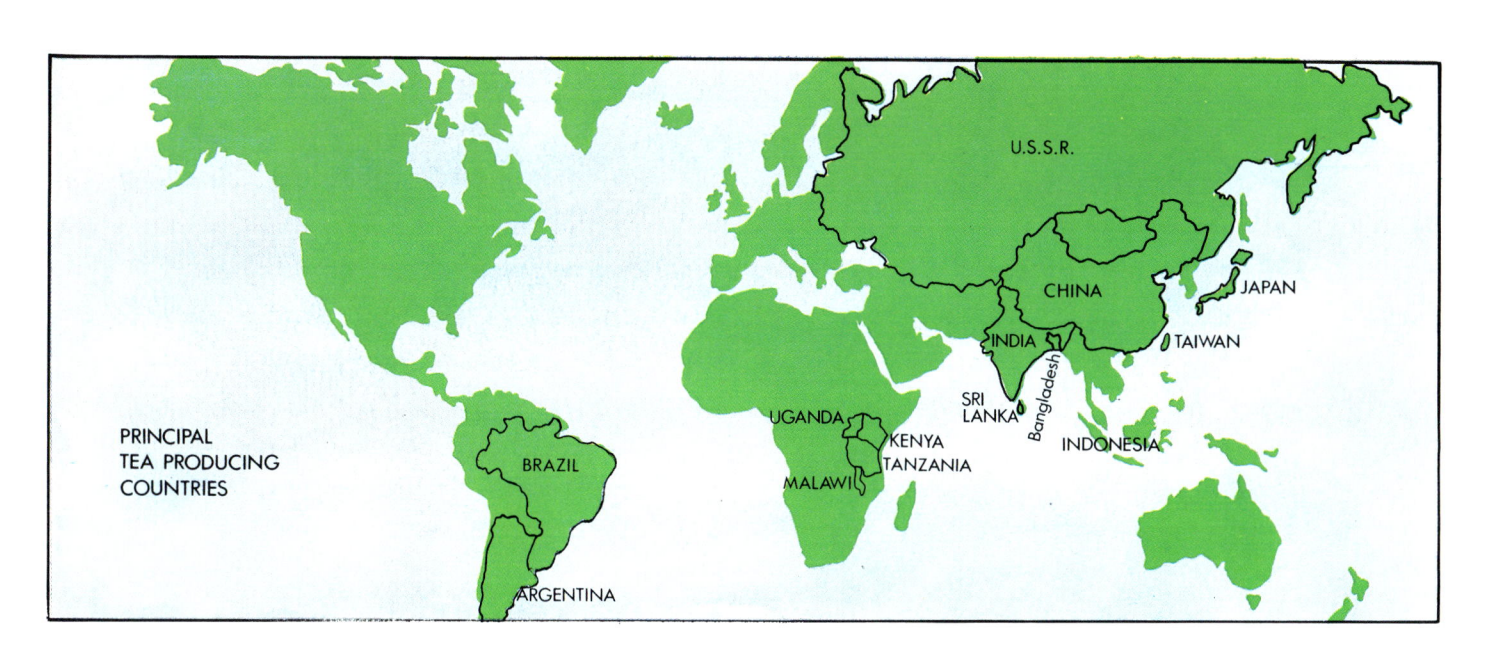

How tea was first discovered

According to legend, the first man to drink tea was a Chinese Emperor, over four thousand years ago. When some tea leaves fell by accident into a pot of boiling soup, they smelt and tasted so delicious that the Emperor drank tea for the rest of his life.

Tea soon became the most important drink in China, and much was written about how to grow and brew it. Bricks of tea were even used for barter. For many centuries the secret of growing and brewing tea remained in China.

A thousand years ago, the Chinese took tea to Japan, but it was still a long time before the drink reached Europe. The first people to bring it to Europe were the Dutch, about 350 years ago. They soon started a tea plantation on the island of Java.

At that time, tea was very expensive to buy, and soon went mouldy because it was not stored properly. So, as soon as it was taken from the ships, it was brewed up and the liquid was kept in huge barrels. Then when some was wanted, it could be drawn off like beer and heated up again.

The growth of the tea trade

Tea quickly became the most popular drink in Britain. It was brought by ship from China, where the British controlled most of the trade. The word 'tea' comes from the Chinese word 'tay'.

The British also sent tea to their colonies in North America. But they demanded a tax on it, which angered many Americans. At the port of Boston, in 1773, some citizens, dressed up as Indians, threw three ship-loads of tea into the sea. This was one of the first incidents in the American struggle for independence, and is known as 'the Boston Tea Party'.

Soon, other countries began to take away Britain's trade with China. The Americans built very fast sailing ships, called 'clippers', which carried the tea around the world much more quickly. So the British, who were well established in India, planted large tea estates there. Indian tea grows faster than China tea, and soon it became the most popular.

As tea growing became a more important industry, the old methods of rolling and drying by hand, which had been used for thousands of years, were replaced by machines. But tea plantations still need plenty of workers to look after the plants and pluck the leaves—there are no machines good enough to do that!

Where to find out more

Next time you go into a food shop, see how many different kinds of tea they sell. The packet will tell you where the tea comes from. To find out more about tea and tea-growing, write to:

The Ceylon Tea Centre
22 Regent Street
London SW1Y 4QD

The Tea Association of the USA
230 Park Avenue
New York

Books to read:

A First Look at Tea by Valerie Pitt
   (Franklin Watts)
Cocoa, Tea and Coffee by H. K. Ashby
   (Wayland)
Tea by Michael Smith
   (Ladybird Leaders)